# *Wide Open, Wild & Willing*

*A Poetry Guide to Discovering
What Is Alive In You Now*

Julia Archer

To the Holy Spirit, who is within me.
To Mother Earth and Father Sky,
who have forever held me.
To John O'Donohue, who speaks with me.

*Harden not your hearts.*
*Love and serve each other.*
– Oma

Cover Art by Paula Ramirez

This collection has lived in me for seven years. It is in your hands now because it must be its own. Yours, even. Make it so. Do not let this book sit on your shelf. Read it aloud. Take the questions, that have been carefully curated over the years to release medicine, and sit with them. Know that you find answers wherever you go searching. You will become the questions you consider.

in the best of loves i have been stretched.
i have felt the rubber band constrict my heart
and i have felt his fingers pull back to stretch
like an arrow, stretch
like the rays of sun upon a blue sky, stretch
like a mother's belly after birth
her skin hanging loose where her baby no longer lies.

in the best of loves I have been broken open
in the best of loves I have cradled the snapped back
hurt of a heart
and told her *you are wider now. you are wider.*

# *LIVING IN ALIGNMENT WITH DESIRE*

*The glory of God is a human being fully alive.*
— Ireneus

*What does being alive mean to you?*

You have been brought here for a specific purpose. No other will ever have your voice, your name, your fingerprints. The way you laugh at the expanse, or the accident. No other will be able to create as you do. Nor share the spirit, the intimacy and the intensity that breathes between you and your siblings, you and your parents, you and your lover. No other will ever know of the sanctity between you and your Lord. As John O'Donohue said, 'To be born is to be chosen.' You chose to be here, in the magic of the sensory world. Each person is a world; a universe. Your true purpose here is to acknowledge what is born in you, what you have been gifted to give, and let it live.

Source is the water, the wellspring, the river.

This earth plane is the rock.

You are the bridge between what is above and what is below.

What lives in you is every emotion that wells out of you.

Fear of feeling causes more suffering than the original feeling itself.

Attempting to hold onto or push away emotions is trying to stop something that is innately designed to flow.

Any fully experienced emotion moves up into a higher vibration.

When you can be with any feeling, you will feel good most of the time.

We get so caught up in wanting to feel happy to be happy to need happy that we forget that in feeling sadness or let down or disappointment we are nourishing the side of the spectrum that will deepen joy. How far down you go is how high you will reach. So the goal must not be to feel happy, because we'll chase it and in the process it will be running away from us, and we'll be running away from pain too. The goal must be, every day, to feel. Anything. To be with those sensations. What our mind deems can or cannot live is not a conversation to our body. It is numbness I fear. Apathy is devoid of spirit, it is inhumane – a death with eyes open. And I will not be anything less than broken wide so the light gets in.

Know now that anything that lives in you is part of you.

Know too, that anything that is born from you is its own

You are here to cultivate integrity, to continue to carve your authenticity.

Your job is to ask questions that bring you closer to the heart of the matter. To the truth.

You are here to shape what is born into what will live.

*All that is born from you will take the form of whatever it is you are.*

You are here to focus only on *being* human.

We were given free will. There is no savior, other than the answer that arises when asking

*What do I desire?* and the action that follows. This is our freedom.

*Desire* comes from the Old French
*desir* and the Spanish word
*decir* means
*to say.*

Our words and our wants are so closely interlinked.

*What is alive in you now?*

Alive: in life. From the Dutch, *liif* means 'body'; *leib* is German for 'womb'; North Frisian's refer to 'limb, person' with *liff,* and the Swedes say *liv* for 'waist'. In Proto-Germanic *lībanq* means 'to remain, stay, be left', and *leyp in* Proto-Indo-European is 'to stick, glue'.

And so, to be alive is to be intensely in the experience of our physical body upon this Earth.

*What a blessing it is
that I can reach
and touch.*

 *This body is a church.*


*How can I be more in my body?*

To *align* is to be in line. When what you *think + feel + do (& say) + the result* all line up.

When you aren't having 'secondhand thoughts' about hopes or worries, then you are connected to the purity of ideas and *heart-led desires* that stem from Source.

Your Intention resides here. To be in the tension. To pull. From the Latin *intentio* 'stretching, purpose.'

Your Intuition is the feelings that come with that thought. Our instruction (our inner structure).

When you do what you say you will do, you are acting in Integrity. From the Latin *integer*, meaning whole or complete.

Your results are the direct expression of your embodied Presence (present: 'now', or 'gift'). When we align our desires with our heads, hearts and hands, we receive the harvest of serving God and others.

Your identity and reputation are built from the consistency of your results. The momentum builds your Essence, which allows you to show up in the now, open wider to new ideas from Source as the process restarts.

I call this *streamlining*.

Thoughts (Intention) + Feelings (Intuition) + Actions & Words (Integrity) + Results (Presence) = all Align (Essence).

*Am I who I need to be for the life I say I want?*
*What am I being called to change in my life?*

You expect a certain result from any action you take. When you complete the streamlining process, you are immediately receiving the in-formation you need in order to act in a better way next time.

This is how simple (I did not say *easy*) it is to live with clarity & magic!

*Do I check in with what I want?*
*Do I ask for what I want?*
*Do I do what I want?*
*Do I get what I want?*

Physical matter is only 0.1% of reality.
Everything you want lives in the unseen.

*All that matters is not yet matter.*

Any state of reality is like a river. I decide to join the flow by diving in, or to sit by the rocks watching others swim by. The current is strong and for as long as I say yes and do the hard and right thing, it takes me where I'm meant to go. The love I bring to another is limited by the love I can bring to myself. I have been on this journey of turning inward. I am relearning how to pray. I am not speaking of religion. I am speaking of asking for what I want and need without agreeing with the narrative that this is a selfish act — simply allowing myself to say what I desire because I must hear it. The alignment of thought, feeling and the word are the first steps to creation. This is true of all things.

*I do not need more than the call of the wind*
*in my bones.*

I live by the Golden Rule:
*Treat others how you would like to be treated.*
And because we live in a mirroring universe, also
*Treat yourself how you would like others to treat you.*

There is no shortcut to wholeness. To be an authentic person is to have direct access to the river of Source.

*How does God speak with you?*
*What does He say?*
*How do you respond?*

When you're looking for answers,
*keep asking questions.*

It isn't about the answers,
the outcome,
the circumstance,
the thing you wanted to happen.

It's about the questions — the
'how am I feeling?' the
'what does this mean to me?' the
'what can happen now?'

Be here. Presence makes certain that your desire stems from the holy, whole and pure place of your Soul speaking. Arrive only with intention so you do not have to return to this moment later to fix it.

Your presence is your essence. We grow away from presence when we choose to follow function over Spirit.

How do you feel when you've been to dinner with friends and they're all on their phones? How do you feel when you've had a three-minute conversation with a stranger who asked you about your life and what you love? It's evident.

The *most* valuable thing in this world is presence. It is an honor and a devotion to the moment, to the relationship taking place.

*We are always after the spirit of things.*

*You are in a constant conversation with life.*
It responds in images, circumstances, other people's voices... in all that appears in the external.
Life is always answering the questions you are asking. What you ask for, you receive.

*Are the questions you are asking wide enough?*

*Invite curiosity.*

There are six questions we can ask: *What? Why? Who? When? Where? How?*

When I focus on wanting the *what*, I am saying I do not have it, and it distances itself from me. Often what I desire will come to me in an entirely different way, place and time than I expected, and I cannot control the *how, when* and *where*.

God's omnipotent perception takes me by surprise. His timing is perfect.

Manifestation. *man*: to embody, *fest*: to celebrate.

To make real in the physical, we must celebrate, have fun, and be joyful. That is what we are asked to do, in three very simple steps:

1. know very clearly what you want
2. know very clearly what it feels like to have that
3. maintain this knowing feeling by connecting with it consistently

As soon as I am certain of the *what*, the shift into the *who* is the magic.

When it comes to bringing my desires into physical reality, embodiment is pertinent. Become the thing you desire. Become the bridge.

It is all resting on *who* it is you are becoming. This is the feeling body: the nervous system.

*Who am I being when I have what I want?*
*What does it feel like to be in his/her body?*
*How does s/he move?*
*How does s/he speak to themselves?*
*How does life work for them?*

I must be the one to take initiative towards my desires by *acting as if* I am the person with the partner, the money, the body, the home. In acting, I am asking. Then the universe speeds up what I set in motion. *The universe matches my momentum.* Fear slows you down. Love speeds you up.

*How would I behave if I knew life was shorter than I think it is?*

Let the circumstances in your life
be the reason you show up.

It isn't about changing your mind.
It's about changing your actions.
Your mind will change with them.

*Why* is the reasoning mind. It keeps me steadfast and moving towards my vision. *Why* is the question that precedes action. It is the fire of motivation, and discipline keeps it burning.

*Why do I want this?*

Ask and answer *why* seven more times. This process will help reach the root of your desire. You will find a larger desire than you first realized was there.

You aren't doing the thing because you don't believe it *needs* to be done. You only *must* do what will expand you in virtue.

It will always make you more magnetic
to have made the decision that is hard today,
but that will make tomorrow easier.

Your subconscious protects you, looks for ways to keep you safe. If expanding will put you at risk, you will not seek to grow. You will not be led to question beyond your means of adaptability.
*How can I make myself uncomfortable next?*
You will have no need.

Create an environment so safe, it begs of you to question. Create a life so aligned, God speaks with you through all appearances.

I asked God for guidance, and He gave me reasons to question my intuition.
I asked God for a partner, and He gave me options to turn away.
I asked God for strength, and He gave me reasons to pray.

What builds a kingdom? The process of choosing what I stand for.

*Decision* and *desire* stem from the same Latin word: *desiderare*. *Decision* comes from the Latin *de-* 'off' and *caedere* 'cut'. To cut off.

When you make a decision, you are going down a path with everything you are; you are cutting off the other option.

Life is a series of decisions. You are always moving closer to or further from what you want.

*You will not love yourself if you do not love your decisions.*

*Do you know how you make decisions?*
Look up your Human Design.
Find out your Authority.
Study your self.

When you decide to stay where you know you don't belong, you go away from what you want. And then what happens? The things that grow *change*. Don't they? The things that grow *move*. They get further away from you. Because you have not decided to follow what you want.

You decide not to grow because you think it will take more than you are willing to or are able to give. But when it is born from love and joy: the more you give away, the more you get.

When you decide to grow, you will no longer have all that you have now.

You will also no longer have all that you have now when you decide to stay where you are.

When you decide to stay with something that has ended you are saying yes to suffering.

You know that it has gone, but you do not want to let go of it.

You must make it more painful to stay where you are than to keep going.

Everyone is getting handled until we are in the mind and heart of God. God is always bringing me back to a life I can fall in love with. Every encounter, person, action, overwhelm, accident — it is all to realign me to my highest path. I see what occurs in the world of change around me not as a failing or a missing or a breaking, but as a *rearranging.*

*God realigns.* He course-corrects. God takes the reins on my heart and guides me to what my Soul knows is meant for me. Every single untrue thing falls away. If it were true, it would not fall. If it were true, it could not fall.

*You* are the constant to change.

Change in the external world is a falling away of all that is not true because *you are the embodiment of truth.*

When you decide to move with the nature of things towards expansion, to dedicate your actions to presence, then you live in the power of the Almighty. Your world is enlarged beyond perceived space and time. You are eternally supported in this stronghold.

Do not be afraid. Life favors the bold and the brave. It rewards the fools who take leaps of faith. Do you adapt to the circumstances life brings you as gifts? Do you jump?

The quality of your life is directly proportional to the risk of the fall.

*How do I want to play here?*
*What can I get away with?*

Know this: you will never regret the doing.

This is our book: *Wide Open, Wild & Willing.* Are you?

# *THE INTENSITY OF THE HEART & THE JOY OF INTIMACY*

John said once that our bodies are in our souls, not the other way around. I believe this. Our Soul is our Aura. And we live in it. Aura. *Au*: the symbol for the element of gold. *Ra*: the Egyptian God of the sun. *Soul* sounds like the Spanish word *sol*, which means sun. The aura, the soul, the golden sun. It is alight.

> *If the body is in the soul*
> *and I am beside you,*
> *then we are in each other's souls.*

The Sacred Heart is the first heart. A whole heart consumed in flame, it is the Divine emblem of risk and faith; the symbol for making beauty out of pain; the perfect balance of soft and hard. Your heart is the hearth. It is from this floor of a fireplace that your golden sun emerges and extends to envelop anyone in a three feet space around you.

When we are in the intimacy (into-me-see) of another's presence we either feel safe or at risk. Our aura is picking up on the information in theirs: the emotions they carry, the weight or the lightness of the load.

The word *empathy* comes from the Greek. Em: in. Pathos: suffering or passion. In feeling. This is where the power lies because feeling is what motivates the meaning we attach to our circumstances.

When I focus on being a wholehearted person –to lead with the heart and the intuition, to fulfill my own needs and desires, to see the darkness and yet decide to stay light– everything outside of me is an extension, an addition, a work of art. I see nothing less than magic.

The heart is the intensity of life.

*How close to the fire do you want to be?*

You cannot find anything outside of yourself.
Reaching distance is only a meter on purpose.
Touch your heart.




Your heart is at your body's center
demanding
to be put first.




You move according to the story you tell yourself.
Tell only the story of how you would like things to
be.

Navigating this human experience has never been about your circumstances.

It has never been about how many times your heart has broken.

Being human is about how many times you allow your heart to break open.

When you fall in love with the journey, it's about how big you can be.

You must know that it isn't the achievement you want — it's the *feeling of success!*

And joy is the greatest rebellion.

I have come to see that everything in life is a relationship.

From the people to the moment to the object.

Every aspect outside of me is in a relationship with me: it responds to me and is created by me in my current environment.

It comes from knowing the response-ability I have in this shared presence.

It is as much my choice to feel love, joy, bliss, as it is my choice to feel sadness, grief, pain.

How I choose to create the feeling in me is through the relationships around me.

When each of these is intimate, I am simply a witness to the greatness.

I choose to wear beautiful clothes every day and to walk to the beach and to do the work so that I can reap the reward. I choose to no longer give to what takes from me.


I choose to be in an intimate relationship with all of life.

*What am I in an intimate relationship with?*

*What/who am I distanced from?*
*Where do I check out in my life?*
*What am I distracting myself from?*
*What hole am I trying to fill by acting in this way?*
*How can I fill this space for me?*

I know the depths of pain and the heights of joy.
We expand in all directions, not only forwards.

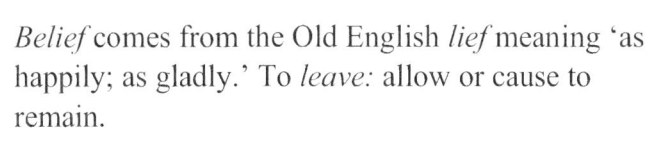

*Belief* comes from the Old English *lief* meaning 'as happily; as gladly.' To *leave:* allow or cause to remain.

We are to do all things in joy, or not at all.

*Reciprocity is the natural state of things.*

You did not come here to feel guilt and shame.
You came here to clear that.

You came here for the pleasure.
You came here for the fun.
You came here to be more like a child: curious, playful, unafraid to try, loud.

You came here for more of the joy.

Negative emotion is a symptom of dis-ease wanting to bring me back to balance; a sign that I'm going against my nature.

*IT'S ALL FOR YOU.*

*What habits bring me the most joy?*
*How can I do more of them?*
*What am I really great at?*
*What comes easily for me?*
*What puts me in a flow state?*

Fall in love with the process.
That is all there is.



As a child, I'll see her from the backseat of the car, the moon, I'll swear she has the face of my grandmother. In her pursuit, I'll think, she has the temper of my father, and I'll be twelve before I figure out she isn't chasing me, never was. At sixteen I'll say my goodbyes to the land from the wing of an airplane and know I am moving towards her. Across the ocean, she will turn her face. But I will be twenty-three, butt naked and peeing by a river in the light she casts the night I see her for the first time. I can never escape her–wouldn't dare. And when telephone lines are so long they share the distance with the shadows back home, she will deliver any message I whisper to her. It is the same moon.



Everywhere I walk I see the light in things.
*What will I do in this holy space?*

Today I stared at the sun
in its first seven minutes as it rose
and in its last seven as it set.

I used to think it housed God, and then I saw Him
in the light of the moon over the water and thought
*No. He cannot only be in one place.*

Joy itself is as light

                        as a feather, as bright

                                            as the sun.

i crack open like a star
and think
*i might take this house up to the sky with me*

She says, *Write it down. Write down how you want to feel.*

I ask,
*How do you spell l a u g h t e r?*
*It is something I can hear*
*and it is something I can see*
*but it is not something I can pronounce.*

She says,

*Show me how you unzip your heart down to your belly button each morning. How you choose to wear the dress that wraps around your hips and opens at your ankles. Show me how the hummingbird kisses the red flowers on the bush beside the stoop where your dad used to bury his cigarette butts. Show me how you wake up with the sky God paints you and how you reach the sea before the waves that touch the sun hit the beach. Show me the bright in your eyes and your open mouth like in a picture as the water brings safety to your feet.*

*And now,* She says, *spell laughter.*

*Even the cliffs give way*
    *to the gentle touch of the ocean*

If all that is good and bright and holy exists in this world, it is because I know it to be true.

Where all is pure, noble, lovely – that is where I am.

*What does who I am becoming choose?*
*What do his/her relationships feel like?*
*How does s/he impact people?*
*How does s/he make things fun?*

Anything we do not hold love for is showing us our own shadow.

*Before you put the stars in the sky, you knew me.*

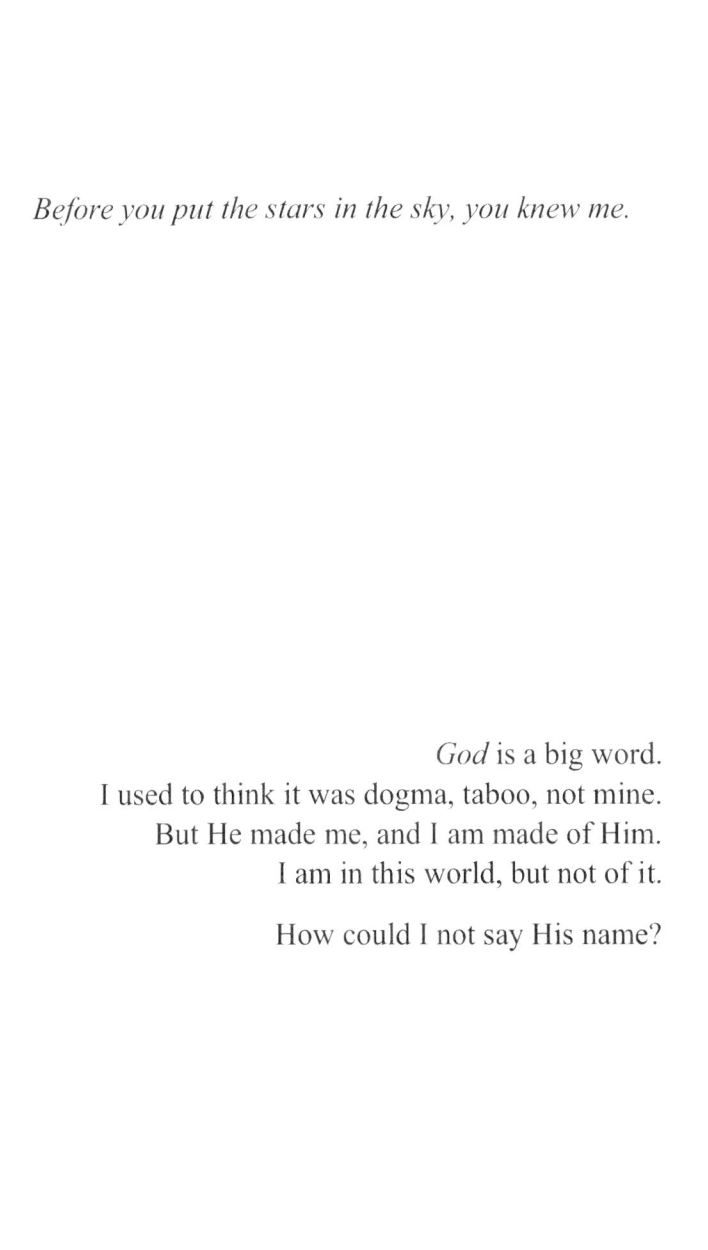

*God* is a big word.
I used to think it was dogma, taboo, not mine.
But He made me, and I am made of Him.
I am in this world, but not of it.

How could I not say His name?

At a petrol station in South Africa
there is a boy called 'Neo'
*And what does it mean?* my mother asks his father
before another stranger answers, *Gift.*

There is a woman at the souvenir store
Whose name tag reads 'Dikeledi'
*Tears*, she says.
*Happy ones?*
*My parents died before I could ask.*

When I am handed my coffee after lunch
I call 'Sbongile' by her name, *Thank you.*

At dinner, *Good evening, you may call me Forgive
and I will serve you tonight* and as she spells her full
name in my notes
'Rivalela' *Forgive*
I see how these people know more than us
'Mikhongelo' *Prayer*
about where we came from.

Your name says everything about you.

Julia means *youthful*,
Christine *follower of Christ*,
Maria *of the sea,*
Archer *all things are good which are honest* &
Strong *the way is tried.*

We are given our name by Source.

When we follow our name's meaning, we are furthering our purpose here.

It is only when you ask
*And what is your art?*
in other words
that you know what a woman is
and what she is capable of.

> Why do birds have wings?
> The closest thing to a dove is a woman.

I'm no angel, but
I can walk into a full room, and I swear
when I'm seen
people either look away
or can't bear to look at all.

When I walk into where it's loud
and speak to the stillness of their souls
like I'm asking their quiet to come out,
it unsettles those who don't know
what that is.

You are made to believe
that if it is quiet, She is not there
when She is in hiding.

She is what gives breath.

      You cannot *force* Spirit to be,
but you can create conditions for It to become.

        Spirit must plant Itself somewhere.
            Be Its roots.

*Do I feel that my relationships show up for me how I show up for them?*

*Do I feel that my relationships show up for me how I show up for me?*

Let it be a slow thing,
this changing.
Allow time to pour over you like honey.
Nothing but softness grows here
and darkness doesn't last.

Oh, what a gift to experience the birth of lightness!
What a joy to become what bright things are!

*Today is the first day of the rest of my life.*

# *A DEVOTION TO TRUTH & PEACE*

Truth is a meaning you repeatedly agree with that forms the basis of your behaviors, which eventually forms your beliefs and identity. *Truth has no need to prove itself, it just is.*

I have yearned for truth desperately, naively, not knowing how much it would take from me to grow, and every time, almost like some masochistic streak, I want it more. Every single time, that rudimental yet impermanent pain is the portal to the miracle, to the blessing, to the joy, to all that is worth something. And in this hunger, in this pursuit, I am asking of truth to show itself. Irrevocably, it does.

*Peace* comes from the Latin word *pax*, 'tranquility', *pacīscor* 'agree, stipulate' and *pangō* 'fasten, fix'. To stipulate a fixed tranquility. A sense of wholeness. And yet *peace* shares pronunciation /pēs/ with its opposite. *Piece:* 'a part of a whole, a fragment'.

Whatever you haven't made peace with is a latent and potent source of power. One that can be used by you to concentrate your essence and open you, or left to confuse your clarity and close you. Transmute.

*Peace is setting the pace.*

Having a peaceful life requires a great amount of *I DO NOT KNOW AND I AM COMPLETELY AND UTTERLY OKAY WITH THAT.*

What is at peace is what is most alive in you. What is at peace burns brightest, for it is in the heart of the hearth.

To access the truth of oneself,
to really know one's potency and medicine,
is to punch holes in the bliss of ignorance for a living.

*If something is not true to me, why do it?*
*If I am not gaining clarity though it, why do it?*

More than once,
when my back ached and my heart wanted to burst,
I took myself to the sea.
I just screamed at her and she took my voice
out of my lungs and almost burst my eardrums and
when the sound stopped
my face was covered in salt and
my body was light as foam.

*Breathe, until quiet and comfort remarry.*

You must get to a place where
the wind does not make a flame flicker,
and the barking dog is a sound.

The only true thing I can do in this life is create,
having faith that what I do will inspire others
to make their own hearts live
in something other than their chests.

the same wind   that lifts   the    heart

                              lets    it         go.

the most powerful creation is beauty

                                    born from pain.

*WHAT YOU BELIEVE TO BE TRUE
WILL BE TRUE.*

*GOD IS WHAT YOU BELIEVE THE TRUTH
TO BE.*

You will find God
wherever you go looking for Him.

That is the danger, or the magic.

I became free
when the list of people
who had power over me read only:

                        - *God*

Meaning is only created within you. Everything external is neutral. If you don't assign meaning to something, it has no value. When I do not assign meaning to what does not bring me joy, it disappears.

*How does this serve me?*

*EVERYTHING SERVES MY HIGHEST GOOD.*

*How does this open me?*

I am given the chance
to do better
with every breath.

Take everything as it comes,
leave everything as it goes.

You are a living vessel.

Only the caverned seek answers externally.
The inner seeker finds an ocean of knowing;
an immediate and everlasting peace.

The greater the world, the larger the power.
Will you grant power to yourself or another?

*Go within*
*so you do not*
*go without.*

The only thing that can be toyed with is your insecurity.
Know its name
so there may be no game.

This old man was sitting next to me at the bus stop, in the shade. We had long to wait, and it was chilly, but he was smiling and whistling. Then he promptly left his spot beside me and went with his cane to stand in the sunlight. He opened up his arms, like a plant, giving everything, taking everything. He opened up his mouth; a silent scream or an attempt of a yawn, I couldn't tell. But that was it: he didn't remain in the shadows where he thought he should stay, he was embracing what was right in front of him, if just across the street.

*If you're looking for peace, it's already here.*

It's in stillness that I recognize what is real. The more present I can be, the more I see things as they are.

What is God feels free.
I anchor in Your peace.

# *ON DISCERNMENT & CONTRADICTION*

When Ego talks, I feel anxious. When Soul talks, I feel at ease. The ego will create chaos and pull you through all the motions. The soul will seek the path of least resistance. The soul gives the ego meaning. The ego protects the soul. They coexist.

*Heaven & hell are places in the mind.*

What happens in any given moment that we do not live with the conscious intention of being heart-led? We lose sight of what's important.

We may lose our temper, bite back at those we love, not hear what they said to us. We may forget something important. If we're further down the line, we may feel entirely distant from the world.

*You sold your soul to the Devil!* they say. It is in losing intimacy, in losing contact with our inner selves, that this process of distance begins. All because we are distracted (to draw apart) from where our bodies are in the present moment. In this world that aims to traumatize, we learn to disassociate. Being broken, forgetful, confused, delusional, argumentative, lost, are devilish traits that cannot amount to anything but a fragmentation of soul.

This is how we let the Devil in: our subconscious installs anything waved past and into our programming. It lives when we are not active in our attention to our hearts, nor standing guard at the gates of consciousness. When inverted, *Devil* spells *lived*. This is all that realm can do: distort, reverse, confuse. It cannot create; only imitate. It perpetuates the pattern of halfhearted living.

*Can you do more with all of you?*

It takes a great deal of courage to remain clear, even if you're the strongest person you know, and the only one who is there for you to feel through it. Because strength is this: holding the space for whatever emotion must come.

Clarity doesn't come from seeking more. It comes from seeing things as they are. Being led by Christ and the Sacred Heart means we are living in wholeness. Others will feel it if you don't do it with all of your body. It is a nervous system thing. It is not only about the language; it is about whether you're saying it with the entirety of who you are.

*People make you feel the way they feel.*

Every single thing that is good *became* so. Order must be made. It is chaos that turns up unprepared. Your power is to be fully in this moment. To remain a whole soul, aware and ready for anything that may arise. You have it all. You are chosen and whole and perfect. Do the work to remain this way.

*I desire to bring light into this world.*

Too many are devoted to disassociation by default. Our culture venerates immaturity. The illusion of progress is the majority. There are few people who choose discipline and difficulty over idolatry and quick hits of dopamine. It takes a wholehearted person to sit with the discomfort of long-term desire. I'm talking about Empire and Legacy.

*STARVE THEM OF YOUR LIGHT.*

Nothing is a greater test of character than when God realigns. Watch them at their most vulnerable; at how they handle hurt. That will tell you who they are.

Choosing to float drifts.
Keep your hands on the helm.

*Always keep the light behind you.*
*You know why? You know where you're going!*
*When I stand beside myself I see so much.*

*– Oma*

*WHATEVER YOU DO IS IN SERVICE TO SOMEONE.*

*Who am I doing this for?*

If it is for others, you will be disappointed again and again. If it is for God, He will make your purpose greater.

Attach your self-worth only to how you do God's work. You won't regret a thing.

*Am I saying this because I want to say it or to receive a response?*
*Where in my life do I rely on external authority or stimulation?*
*What if everything I expect from others I do for myself?*
*Am I more likely to break a promise than to live untruly? Why?*

*Do you know what God sounds like when He speaks with you?*
*What/who do you trust?*
*Who is your God?*

Never let another decide what God you serve.
Your power is expensive.

Do not make the mistake of assuming that every heart is like yours. You do not know who they defend.

Do not be so daring as to put your faith in places you cannot control.

I know that my connection to God
is the strongest there is.
I know that your connection to God
is the strongest there is.
I will not get in the way of your ability
to be God's hands & feet.

We ground Him on this Earth.

We hold ideals on how things should look/feel/be. But thoughts and feelings are only half of the alignment process. It is deceptive to appear. Not all things are absolute. Nuance lives in the details and opposes absolutes. Sometimes we must adapt to life's situations to reach the desired outcome; bend so we do not break. Sometimes no matter what happens we couldn't have done better. You couldn't have predicted it. You are always adapting to the set of circumstances that show up in front of you at that time. That is the point. Do not marry what is rigid to flexibility before you know what the occasion will ask of you. Both the structure and the flow are required.

*Am I pulled towards this?*
*Does this feel expansive or contractive?*
*Am I receding or am I reaching?*
*Will this make tomorrow easier or harder?*
*How easy can this be?*

*The difference between a beautiful thing
and a thing of beauty is that the first appears;
the other breathes.*


There will forever be levels of deception
masquerading as beautiful things.

*Am I escaping or facing something difficult by taking
part in this?*

No avoidant person self-reflects.


All that is for me is to do what God asks of me.
Identifying as 'spiritual' is the ego perpetuating itself.
It is not for me to tell you who I am. That is for you to
decide. To say you are something is to be it less.


Beautiful things don't ask for attention.
Allow things to speak for themselves. They do.

I do not want in on this world
that searches into the night for what I find
at the beach; that stays awake until the time I leave
sleep, in pursuit; that fills up another glass
for a crack of a smile
when my fuel is the silence
between saying.

I do not want in on this world
that soaks in bitterness
and expects
a taste of sweet.

> I cannot be holy, nor love,
> if I do not have chaos or wreckage;
> if I do not harbor brokenness until it does not hurt.
>
> One cannot exist without the other.

Choose who you open your heart to wisely. Do not put another fallible human between you and Source. When you place another on a pedestal they turn into a God. What you deify has power over you.

You only are what you focus on.
When you hate something, you become like it.
When you love something, you become like it.

If you aren't full of something, you aren't that.
Overwhelm yourself with it!
Obsess over it!
Let it overflow!

*Are you attached to who you think you are?*

How many *I*'s have I been?
How many *you*'s have I loved?

                    Sometimes crying is not grieving
                    and loving is not widening and
                          beauty is not lasting.







Redefine *perfection*
as a wholeness.
As a holding of two sides; all sides.
Perfection cannot be one-sided.
It could not only hold strengths and 'goodness'.
Perfection is entire: whole and holy.
There is only the All appearing as this:
complete & perfect.

# *ON FAITH & FATE*

Recently I've been thinking of the concept of fate, that my life has already been written. It's because of the stars that I am given opportunities and that certain feelings arise or fall away. But I get to play with what patterns to begin or end or recreate.

What if it's all preordained? What if whatever I choose is exactly what was going to happen? This is why it is said that *everything happens for a reason*: to create as has been created.

In this sense, the present is the past.

This makes me feel so *safe*. No matter what feelings I have now, I will get there: to the end. Whether I like it or not, I will have heartbreak and failure and forgetfulness; and I will have greatness and success and love. Until I get there, *how* I do so is the game.

*What if what I want is inevitable?*
*What would I do?*
*How would I walk?*

*Everything happens to align you with your destiny.*

It is written that I will find the path meant for me and what I am to say in this world before I leave it. It is written that I shall be a mother and have children and take all the women God wills with me through motherhood. It is written that I shall love many and lose lots, but it is through love that I'll have lived at all. It is written that I'll take the stories to my grave, but not before I have shared them, and many others do the same. It is written that I will have found the love of my life by twenty, when it is pouring down on a caravan roof and I am singing into the voice recorder on my phone, when I am made homeless and have nowhere else to go near winter, and then still it is written that the love of my life is with me from conception.

I know this for I have lived it and will continue to live into the worded days, the sentenced years.

*My fears have been dwarfed by my fate.*

*Is there such a thing as an afterlife? When we pass, do we ever come back?*

*Yes, I think there is an afterlife. And we do come back. In so much as our souls are one. We came from Source and will return to it. We came to this planet in these bodies and will return in new ones when we are ready. Neither you nor I will come back. But we are the same: you are a part of me and I of you. Like the waves belong to the ocean.*

> All that begins
> completes itself
> and may spiral.

It's in not knowing what will come
that the will to become is born.

*How does God design every single circumstance that leads me to make the decisions I make?*

They say that *not every plan will turn out as expected* because they aren't devoted to God's plan. Most people sit in the sand trying to hold onto it. That is not what we were given.

Our sensory perceptions are unbelievably limited, and we do not see how ends meet. We get stuck in the feelings of things and assign meaning to the *act* before the *result* has come to pass. We hand over our power before the streamlining process is complete. Feelings are solely the second step and are transient in the building of Legacy. God saw the outcome before it began.

I decided long before I came into this world that I would experience what I am now saying yes to, and what I do not expect. I asked God for the hard lessons and am beyond thankful for them. They are the reason I change. If it were easy, I would not change. My soul knows I need to feel a painful thing to avoid choosing it again.

But how could I have wanted something that isn't good?

I did not sign up for the momentary pain or glory. I signed up for the truth: for growth, for strength, for courage, for wisdom, for resilience. I signed for the morals, for the outcome, for the result; for a more potent presence and essence.

All that I hold onto with dear faith in this life is in God's hands. I am attached only to what God is already holding: my trials and my blessings and my miracles.

Then I don't have to worry about sand slipping through my fingers because I wasn't holding onto that sand in the first place. I'm just glad I'm in the water.

*hold onto the truth*

*the meaning you can make of it*

*hold onto your mind*

*your body*

*your soul*

*turn hurt into joy*

*Lead by example.*
*Show the Divine what vessels to pour into.*

The light and the shadow live in every expression of physical reality.

Learning a deeper truth will rid you of the prior deceit, but lasting transformation is sure to arrive with the birthing pain of acceptance. Becoming a new person brings its own fears.

There is no place without limitation. There is only the choice to live open to a faux freedom that keeps you closed, or open to the point of expansion that even the sky yearns for. There is only the choice to remain unaware of what is happening without your knowledge, or to break open onto the floor above on which God lives. To surrender to every way the river of truth flows is to say yes to the fear of surprise for where the current will take you.

*How has my capacity to surrender increased?*

*TRUST IS A GROWING THING.*

It does not matter what path you choose;

it matters who you are being while you are walking.

You can use anything as your process.

Make sure it is a worthwhile thing,

an honest thing,

a holy thing.

You will know it is when it makes you more that way.

Choose a process as close to the heart as possible

like writing, for the arms are but an arms-length away.

Or speaking even; the arms are but an extension of the heart.

Whatever it is, make it loud and craft it through you.

I want to see your spirit alive in all you touch.

*The walls you walked past yesterday – they're golden.*

I finally understand the pattern of life.
That is not to say
that I am not moved by it.



Life always comes full circle, and it is only when ends meet that it makes any sense. Endings, although painful, are as sacred as beginnings. There are many different sizes of circles: some lay on top of each other and some swallow others and others still lay latent and miniature like a stone or a full stop separate from all the rest and if we're lucky someday they spiral concentrically, but the point is that beauty is inlaid into difficulty and joy is a curve in the line of disappointment and there was never a person who once had to forgive and smiled again without thinking *when will this end? how bittersweet life is! it grants us what we do not want for a short time only, and it grants us for a short time only more than we could wish for.*



*It all leads to itself.*

*Fall, reach, grab, pull, laugh. Fall, reach, grab, pull, laugh. Fall, reach, grab, pull, laugh. Fall, reach, grab, pull, laugh. Fall, reach, grab, pull, laugh. Fall, reach, grab, pull, laugh. Fall, reach, grab, pull, laugh. Fall, reach, grab, pull, laugh. Fall, reach, grab, pull, laugh. Fall, reach, grab, pull, laugh. Fall, reach, grab, pull, laugh. Fall, reach, grab, pull, laugh. Fall, reach, grab, pull, laugh. Fall, reach, grab, pull, laugh. Fall, reach, grab, pull, laugh. Fall, reach, grab, pull, laugh. Fall, reach, grab, pull, laugh. Fall, reach, grab, pull, laugh. Fall, reach, grab, pull, laugh. Fall, reach, grab, pull, laugh. Fall, reach, grab, pull, laugh. Fall, reach, grab, pull, laugh. Fall, reach, grab, pull, laugh. Fall, reach, grab, pull, laugh. Fall, reach, grab, pull, laugh. Fall, reach, grab, pull, laugh. Fall, reach, grab, pull, laugh. Fall, reach, grab, pull, laugh. Fall, reach, grab, pull, laugh. Fall, reach, grab, pull, laugh. Fall, reach, grab, pull, laugh. Fall, reach, grab, pull, laugh. Fall, reach, grab, pull, laugh. Fall, reach, grab, pull, laugh. Fall, reach, grab, pull, laugh. Fall, reach, grab, pull, laugh. Fall, reach, grab, pull, laugh. Fall, reach, grab, pull, laugh. Fall, reach, grab, pull, laugh. Fall, reach, grab, pull, laugh. Fall, reach, grab, pull, laugh. Fall, reach, grab, pull, laugh. Fall, reach, grab, pull, laugh. Fall, reach, grab, pull, laugh. Fall, reach, grab, pull, laugh. Fall, reach, grab, pull, laugh. Fall, reach, grab, pull, laugh. Fall, reach, grab, pull, laugh.*

*Life is a burning down // into*

You will always receive your lowest standard. Your shortcomings. Our hopes lead our words, and our fears lead our actions.

Make your hopes more painful to lose than your fears are pleasant to keep.

The more you can meet your fears, the more you will perform according to your hopes.

Before you are given what you've asked for you will be tested. *Here's the thing that comes dressed as everything you want.* And then you deny it because you know that isn't yours, yours feels different, and you carry on living your big life, and the fully formed thing comes along and you don't even stop to recognize it, it just floats into your way one day and you're walking the path a while before you look back like *Oh! That's when I got blessed!* All because you cleared, you flowed, you remained true to your vision of who you are and what you deserve: nothing less than your biggest self.

There's a kid standing outside a pub. He's holding a piece of paper, a drinks menu or something, between two fingers. It's folded up jaggedly, like a concertina, but with a tail and wings and– it's an airplane, a paper airplane. So he's holding this paper plane like a spirit level, checking that all its parts are balanced, that they're all even, all okay, all *right*. He's gripping it like a pen now: poised, pointed skyward. His glasses are magnifying his eyes and he's looking at it just– *needing* it to take off. Willing it to. And so he throws it. He throws it as far away from him as he can, his whole arm stretching out, his joints straight, his fingers strained, the plane flies out of his hand and it just spirals to the ground. He picks it up and he throws it, and he picks it up and he throws it and he throws it and I think *No one tell that kid it's never going to fly.*

You already know what to do.
You already see where you are heading.
You already have what you once wanted.
In presence, you are all-ready.
When He calls you, He equips you.

No matter how afraid you are of it,
go towards your power.
No matter how afraid you are of it,
go towards the truth.

You are prepared.

*Life gifts presence in her process.*




Living is
moving like you have something to die for.

Living is asking
*Is this the closest I'll ever get to me?*

Living is the dance between the calm of the moment
and the chaos of the coming one.

Living is redefining truth daily
so that meanings shorten and silence.
Some end in song.

Your ancestors,
your future children,
and every being resting in the realm
of the imaginary, of non-duality,
are witnessing you.

It is with that truth that you breathe.
It is with that power that you move.

When you haven't been

        listening

                to   the   nudges

                        you'll get        pushed.

      God will increase your urgency.

*we're sitting where the water lives,*

*watching the coastline.*

*God is here*

*in this color of the afternoon*

*right at the edge of the mountain.*

*How could He not be?*

'Cielo' is Spanish for *sky* & *heaven*.
When I breathe,
I am letting heaven in.




*God is dancing with(in) me.*




                               I am centered
                        in the sensory feelings
                        of the present moment.

Each time I have wanted and thought I've known

I'm asked to let go, made to make whole

of the notion of nothing, then something returns;

makes new. It's in the process

of confusion that it is demanded of me

to hold still to truth,

to welcome the possibility of another end

to come through.




There is a power that pulls.

The risks I take
are a series of blind rises
and I'm gifted
a marvelous view.

Keep on lifting.

# *FOR BOUNDARIES & SOVEREIGNTY*

Here's to seeing clearly. Here's to being taken by what and who I want to be given back by. Here's to witnessing all the women who put up boundaries to protect their peace and those they love.

This is the battle and the commitment: to self. Anything beyond the self is just that: an appearance.

If you were made to feel beaten before you entered the conversation, dignity was never held by the other in the first place. Not at the esteem at which you hold it. It isn't about who has the last say. Dignity is about who walks away with less to carry, with set-back shoulders, head high. Dignity is about walking away so you keep standing for what you believe to be right.

When you fall out of wholeness, you can be held to that. People poke at you with their patterns to see when they can bait you back into your own bad behavior. Your job is to remain whole.

Sister: *It's hard to stand your ground when nobody around you does.*

Me: *That's when you must.*

*YOU ARE*

*HOW YOU SHOW UP*

*WHEN IT GETS HARD.*

*What does who you are becoming no longer tolerate?*
*What is s/he unapologetic about?*

If you are not doing your best
in every area of your life,
you are not allowed to point.

Hold your own.

*You don't get what you want,*
*you get what you tolerate.*

It's how I hold myself that I demand you hold me too.

I set the rules.
You follow.

Come to me

with intention

and in wholeness

or do not come.

I grew up with an absent father, an alcoholic, a smoker, and throughout life I projected the care I so desired from him onto father figures. They gave me the talks and mentored me and instilled the values in me I wanted. That my father's limitations ended before my wants began did not mean I had to keep a distorted experience of the masculine. And today, after years of rebuttals, I'm laughing with him.

All present relationships are due to primary relationship patterns. I have the relationship I have with women because of my relationship with my mother. I have the relationship I have with men because of my relationship with my father.

*What is the purpose of this interaction or relationship?*
*Am I being my role?*

The more you cut something
the stronger it grows.




                        It is in the protection of what is

                                  as it is

                        that we remain on holy ground.

## *THE GRIEF OF HURT & THE FEAR OF DEATH*

As a child, when the world seemed one of endless possibility, and upon turning out the light, I used to run from the dark of the downstairs. My young mind would dream up all the monsters she'd seen in the movies and read in the books and summon them then and there. She would run and she wouldn't stop until she made it to the safety of the bed: feet no longer near the floor and head tucked beneath the blankets.

We befriend Dark before we are cells, we meet there, grow there, like a seed sown in soil, in the succor of our mother's womb. Not unlike the eternal flame of faith and breath and heartbeat, darkness meets us first at conception. Dark is the eternal friend. I close my eyes and it is in Dark that everything begins, that anything I imagine is most definitely true, most definitely real.

Tantric teachers tell of Shiva, the divine man, and Shakti, the divine woman: how light found a place to inhabit, how She had found in Him a space to be. Conjure, enchantment, spell work, divination, it is all done in darkness. *All that exudes power demands creation, and quiet.* The common beginnings of a blank canvas, then, are truly black. Black does not ask of you to bring it color – it is already there. What wants to live is already within the black. We are to erase so what always was is allowed to become. In doing so, the light is born.

*Each day,* said another teacher, *you are born again. Welcome the night as if it is death. Then you will live your first, last, only and best day of your life.* Darkness brings permission. In welcoming undesirable feelings that want to come through in sitting with them or in naming them, something remarkable happens: *they move with you.*

Quantum physics tells us that what is observed changes its behavior; that having a watchful eye on one focus makes it almost self-aware. When a double-consciousness occurs, we co-create with all that is. Open arms enable a flow, a movement of joy and sorrow. As they are seen, they pass. It is in truly looking at them for what they are that they arrive where they have meant to go: straight to our hearts. When we open the doors wide, no matter the cost, we are saying *it is safe to be here, it is safe to be.* This makes for a vastly more graceful experience, as they will not come knocking later at unsoundly hours, and we shall not hope one day they might. We grant them the presence they deserve in the dignity we currently hold, and in that freedom, they leave without ill faith. They are transmuted into that genuine beauty that can only be found in dark places.

And so I turn, arms outstretched, towards an unlit living room and go looking for what I do not know, but will absolutely find.




When God rearranges, I hold on for dear life.

But what I love has already died.

I have felt the weight of a dead thing, how

it burdens, it slows, it stalls.

And I am holding this dead thing, trying to laugh.

It wants to be mourned;

let go.

*Nothing I own belongs to me. Nothing I own belongs to me. Nothing I own belongs to me. Nothing I own belongs to me. Nothing I own belongs to me. Nothing I own belongs to me. Nothing I own belongs to me. Nothing I own belongs to me. Nothing I own belongs to me. Nothing I own belongs to me. Nothing I own belongs to me. Nothing I own belongs to me. Nothing I own belongs to me. Nothing I own belongs to me. Nothing I own belongs to me. Nothing I own belongs to me. Nothing I own belongs to me. Nothing I own belongs to me. Nothing I own belongs to me. Nothing I own belongs to me. Nothing I own belongs to me. Nothing I own belongs to me. Nothing I own belongs to me. Nothing I own belongs to me. Nothing I own belongs to me. Nothing I own belongs to me. Nothing I own belongs to me. Nothing I own belongs to me. Nothing I own belongs to me. Nothing I own belongs to me. Nothing I own belongs to me. Nothing I own belongs to me. Nothing I own belongs to me. Nothing I own belongs to me. Nothing I own belongs to me. Nothing I own belongs to me. Nothing I own belongs to me. Nothing I own belongs to me. Nothing I own belongs to me. Nothing I own belongs to me. Nothing I own belongs to me. Nothing I own belongs to me. Nothing I own belongs to me. Nothing I own belongs to me. Nothing I own belongs to me. Nothing I own belongs to me. Nothing I own belongs to me. Nothing I own belongs to me.*

*You were made to hold, not carry.*

Be married to truth,
devoted to expansion,
and only your dead parts will be left in the past.

You can do nothing with them anyway.

You saw all that my lightness was and lifted,
like I climbed down to touch your pain.

You have two choices with your sorrow:
give it up to me and I'll stay.
Make me dig for it, and I'll bury the dirt in your grave.

Grief is love with nowhere to go.

The most liberating things are scary.

You either quit or keep going. They both hurt. I am afraid of giving away my power. My power to choose. So I choose to expand in all directions, into the best version of myself. I am not afraid of an end I cannot control. I am afraid of the one I can. I make every decision to walk straight into my fears daily. The more often I do, the better I get at it. And the process is feeling. Why do so many of us shy away from feeling? Feeling sadness feeling joy feeling ecstasy feeling pleasure feeling anger feeling! This is the human. The risk of the fall equals the rise of the gain. Take the leap. Do the thing that scares you. Tt means you'll fall deeper; it means you'll lift higher too.

*What are you afraid of?*
Then ask *why?* seven times.
When you welcome fear, ask it:
*What is the worst that can happen?*
*How can I move with this fear instead of away from it?*

*ORDEM E PROGRESSO.* There's a mural of a Brazilian flag on the wall behind us. I'm telling you about the ways of this world and how the reaches of joy are polar in their pain — run just as deep only the other way. It is an evil I would rather not imagine and detest that I understand. You look at me like the lights went on all at once in a fairground: wonder and disbelief. *How can you believe such things, they could not possibly be true!* But you aren't laughing at me, like another You did. It is a shock in the shape of a smile that haunts your face. I know. You then speak with simple sincerity when you say I must not sink here. That it is not a place to spend my time — that I am already the light. You say something like that.

And I sit now, alone, like I said I needed to do, and write: *Why do I mourn the things that have yet to leave?*

I think it is human, and let myself be close with strange people who turn out not to be the light I see. I return to the places I've been and realize I don't belong there anymore. I know that to mourn the things that have yet to leave means they may as well not be here. My own body, my own mind, my own soul. I am not afraid of death; I am afraid of not being human. I am afraid of not feeling. Of wasting my time in comfort.

And then there's something measured about the way another You speaks to me. Emotion is kept at bay; like all that wants to be said has been considered. You say it seems I'm on the right path. That I seem 'aligned'.

I'm so pleased it seems that way. There are days I believe you. Sometimes I cry when I'm happy and laugh when I'm sad though no one has explained to me that is healthy. So I cry at your impression of me, and then I laugh.

But it isn't about the standards I set, it's about the ones I live in. I am having a human experience and this vessel belongs to God. He has a way of gifting me things I have returned to Him. I drop my baggage at his door.

# *FORGIVE RESENTMENTS & LIGHTEN THE LOAD*

To resent. From the obsolete French *resentir: re-*again, *sentir*: to feel. To feel again. To reopen the wound. When you resent yourself or another, you carry a heavy burden, and hold a grudge against your Creator. The conscious mind is meant to engage with the present moment. The subconscious/God is meant to carry the weight of any adverse thought or condition. The conscious mind is limited and cannot think its way out of the present situation; it must give up control.

It is a violation of the law to carry a burden, because we are not then living in the plenty that *is* eternally and abundantly gifted. To worry is a sin. We are here to enjoy (be in-joy) and to fulfill the purpose we were chosen for. That is our obligation.

*YOU DO NOT HAVE TO EARN THE PLACE YOU HAVE BEEN GIVEN.*

It's all about where you hold your sorrow. Do not let your mind or your body carry it. Let your soul have it, for that is a direct link to God. Do you instruct your sorrow to go there? Anything God carries is amplified in the power of love. Do you let Him take it?

You must admit. You must ask. Out loud. *God, will you take my pain? Please, I cannot carry it.*

It is only then that it dissolves; that it becomes something else, as if a fire has turned it to smoke.

Pain gets stuck in the body after a shock or a conflict arises. Pain shows us where we shortcut and what we avoid. Pain brings us back to the present.

German New Medicine (the full database found online) allows us to find the root cause of the pain, and to return it to the soul, where it can live as joy. When it arrives in the soul, it is laid to rest. It is at peace. Joy goes straight there. Joy is charged with a lightness that pain is not.

You have made peace with an emotional situation when you can speak of it out loud without an emotional reaction. You have placed it in your soul then.

*How can you welcome yourself if you deny a feeling?*

*Sanctify:* to free from sin. *Purify*: to remove contaminants from; to make ceremonially clean. Declare holy; *consecrate*. Make sacred (connected to God).

This is your power. All that is holy starts here.

Every person I have ever loved
is grieving too much or a lot
for the things that they are.

How to be a whole person:
1. *Trust* that the energy you feel is real.
2. *Know* that you are always learning the lesson you are meant to be learning.
3. *Pause*. Say thank you for being triggered. Respond.
4. *RELEASE IN EVERY STEP OF THE PROCESS.*

*whole people*
*heal people.*

*What are you ready to let go of?*

How do you feel? And I don't mean right now. I mean how do you let yourself be sad? How do you work through it and then look yourself in the eye and say *I did that?* Tell me how you become happy again. How you sort through everything and decide that actually this is something you want to fight for. Not only your life but all the good things in it. The things that take time. The little details like the napkins being folded on the table or saying *I love you* once more than necessary and showing it tenfold, despite her knowing it. Don't you dare stop yourself from being sad when you have to be. Strength is built, vertebrae by vertebrae. Do not deny yourself.

*What ails you?*

Give me your fear.
Give me your hurt.
Give me your worst.

When you are more than what is soft,
let me see all of you.

I'll be damned to only have half of you.

Can you look at me and tell me

*There is nothing in me that causes pain.*
*Nothing I cannot or am not willing to talk about?*

It's okay to feel like you can't.
As long as you remember you're wrong sometimes.
And this may be one of those times.




I forgive myself
for knowing what I wanted
and acting like I didn't.



                               And despite it all, here we are
                                           laughing.

Write a Ho'oponopono letter to yourself or to someone you hold hurt for. *I'm sorry // Please forgive me // Thank you // I love you*

I'm so sorry for any pain I caused you. I would never wish for any harm to come upon you.

Please forgive me for anything that weighs heavy on you. Please forgive me for all of it.

Thank you for showing me how to be fierce, thank you for seeing every part of me that I didn't see myself, thank you for believing in me. Thank you for making me ask for what I need. Thank you for your company, and for cherishing my body. Thank you for slowing me down. Thank you for loving me. Thank you for allowing me to be devoted to you. Thank you for welcoming me into your world. I really loved being there with you. Thank you for widening mine.

For a time, we were each other's island. You gave me so much happiness. I only wish you the same.

I love you. I have nothing else to leave you with.

I feel the need to say this until it spills out of my soul.

i will always have love for you.
isn't that a beautiful thing?
there will always be love in the places i look

# *ON HOLDING UP THE MIRROR IN LOVE*

Rather than labeling it as one generic feeling, the Ancient Greeks categorized love into eight definitions. First, there is *eros*. Associated with the physical body, this is sexual and romantic love. Next is *philia*, affectionate love or friendship; and *storge*, the love felt between parent and child. *Ludus* is the playful love that has us giggling like children. I find *mania* –linked to our survival instinct– to be the cultural expectation of what love is: a falling-and-wanting-to-be-caught due to its obsessive nature and high likeness to insanity. It is the breeding ground of codependency. Compromise, tolerance and patience are found in the enduring love of mature marriage called *pragma*. Knowing that you cannot give what you do not have, the Greeks deemed *philautia* the word for self-love: a full sense of compassion for one's own soul. Finally, there is *agape*: the unconditional love for the other, the boundless compassion free of expectation, the selfless love of the spirit.

Agape feels like shivers on my skin,
like a thousand raindrops that don't wet,
like the sun is in my belly.
I have faith in nights.



A good friend told me once that a relationship is not only one, but three:

1. between you and that person
2. between him and himself
3. between you and yourself

*You are your own earth.*
You cannot look inside of another for where to stand or drink or breathe.
*Everything is born from me, or it is not born.*




Other than my own connection to source,
there is nothing more sacred than the joy that can be created between two people.

I was once swept up for months by a man I had placed on a pedestal, leaving myself below him. I was in the thralls of blinding love when I let my youthful, happy self go.

When your heart closes, it shows in numbing ways. You appear to most as you did before; it is the intensity of feeling that is missing. The intimacy of being open is what makes us feel alive. This is why we say in hindsight 'I was dead inside.' To return to the viscerality of the now feels like a rebirth.

It is a series of choices that led me to sitting on the sofa one day in June, my sister's heart breaking for me. I broke her trust after I severed my relationship with my own desires. I learned that if you act on another's desires before voicing your own, you are placing the relationship between both of you last.

It was my sister who had me hear what my soul was whispering all along: *You are not* you *right now,* she said. Nothing *feels better than safety.* She did not have to tell me this. She told me that she did not want to. But she felt she had to. And I love her with the world that I remain for her intervention.

Love is telling the truth when it hurts because it will hurt more to hear it later. Any form of self-compassion can only arise in an environment of self-responsibility. The only expectation we can meet is our level of sincerity with ourselves. All actions of self-love fall away *when I need them most.* This is why we have the people who love us looking where we cannot see, watching our blind spots, being painfully honest. It was my sister too who said: *You only learn in spaces where you feel held in the process of not knowing.*

You cannot get to where you need to be on your own.

Why do I let what I love get smothered?

You can only ever be near what you love.
If you drop the lines, share its circle, become of it,
it takes on another shape.
Staying at a distance is the closest you can get
for what you love to remain.

*That place where you are? Nobody can get there.*

– Oma

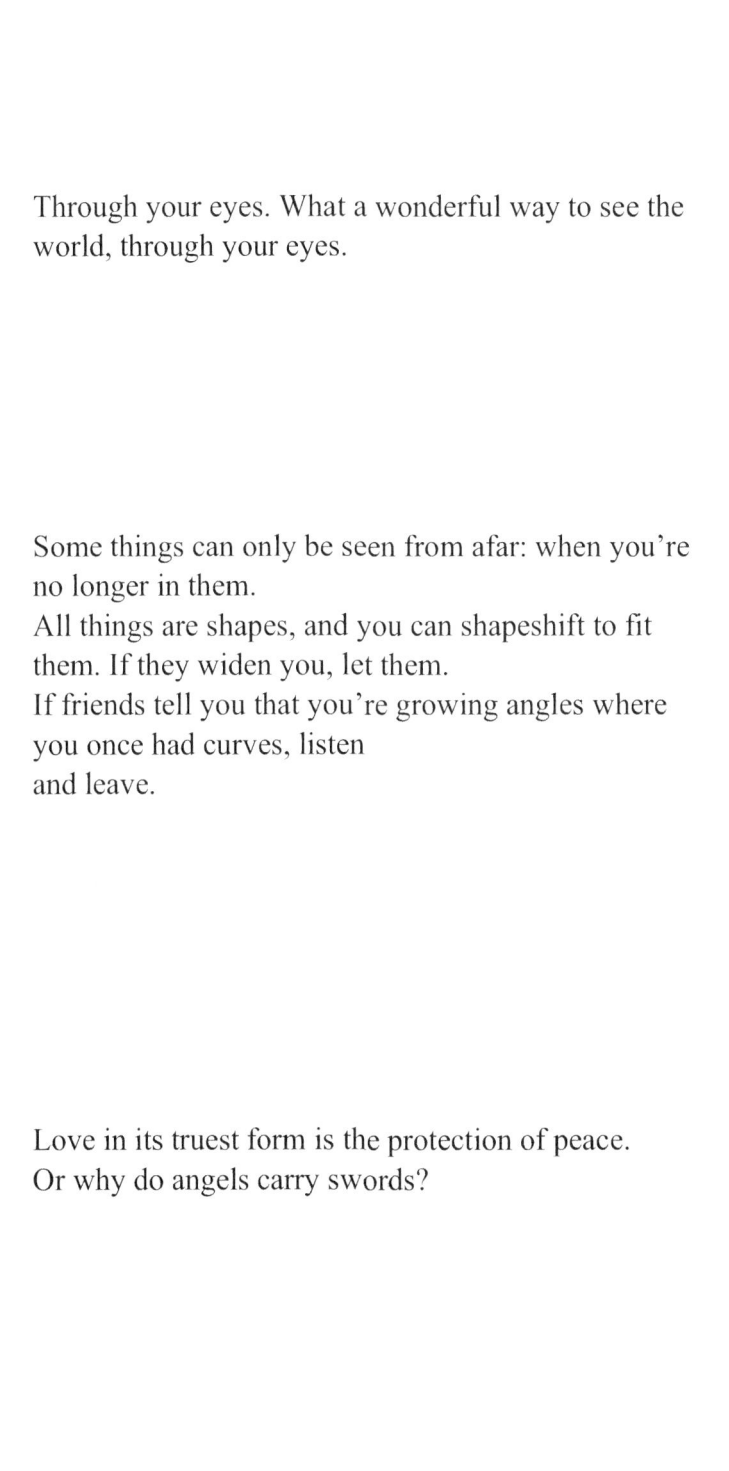

Through your eyes. What a wonderful way to see the world, through your eyes.




Some things can only be seen from afar: when you're no longer in them.
All things are shapes, and you can shapeshift to fit them. If they widen you, let them.
If friends tell you that you're growing angles where you once had curves, listen
and leave.




Love in its truest form is the protection of peace.
Or why do angels carry swords?

Love is all that is given freely; it is what makes you feel alive and in a state of fullness.

I think love is this pure knowing of completion.

*WHATEVER YOU LOVE YOU LEAP INTO.*

I've fallen in love with men
who were not alive when I thought I heard
a breath. It was my own spirit.

And all of it,
I don't want to bring it here, to you.
It is too much of what this is not.
And this is a good thing.

*You show me what the reaches look like.*

Every story has a beginning, a middle and an end, only not in that order. Sometimes the end is first — when love is rushed. Love cannot be rushed. Love comes when it is ready or it never does. Not every story ends well. And by that I mean not every story starts well. The middle sometimes sounds like the silence before the bass drops; or the revving before the cars pull off; or the hum of floating underwater. Some people, some stories, aren't meant to last longer than a few hours. They might be the big red button that says *Why did you give up on that? You're good at that!* and eject us back. They might remind us of what we want *(I WANT LOVE I CAN LIVE WITH NOTHING LESS)*. They might not be meant to tell us more than how they need to shut their eyes with how bright we light up the room. They might remind us of our worth. Never confuse what you're offered with what you deserve.

Love is not attachment. Love is not games, it is not pain, it is not suffering. Love cannot give what it does not have. Love does not exist in another. Love is not denying ourselves for each other. Love is not self-sacrifice.

Love is not given and received;
it is simply discovered and allowed.

Love is always there.

*It is my priority*
*now and always*
*to be the best lover I ever had.*

I don't know what it is
you stir in me
or if I am to move with it,
but I want to.

*Love always makes the first move.*

I have seen more faith in airport Departures than I have in churches. I have been to enough city centers and waiting rooms and staff rooms to know that where the people are is to be consecrated. I have drunk the blood of Christ and eaten His body plenty in the past to know that holding hands is true holy communion. I have seen the face of God in flesh, and heard His voice in a sigh under the covers. Being human is a sacred thing.

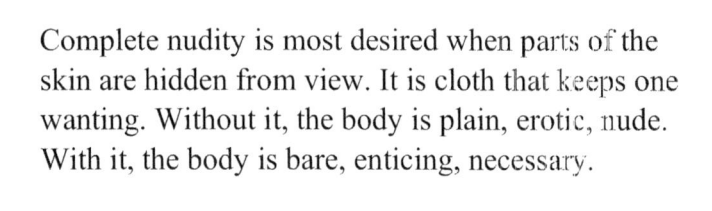

Complete nudity is most desired when parts of the skin are hidden from view. It is cloth that keeps one wanting. Without it, the body is plain, erotic, nude. With it, the body is bare, enticing, necessary.

Love is,
in the fullness of fault and virtue,
an embrace.

*My love for you is deliberate.*

I still have every love I ever had.
People go, but what they left
stays.

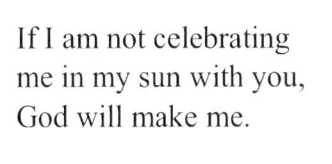

If I am not celebrating
me in my sun with you,
God will make me.

Like the sky at night,
it isn't about how lasting, but about how wide
your love can be for one another. And if that love is
willing, like the depths of the ocean,
to let go of its want for land.

*I give you everything I have and am left with so much
more.*

There's this really big tree outside my window and it's still and large and green –the kind of green you find an overripe avocado goes or maybe the stain on some shorts after a rugby game– that kind of green. Rich and fierce. Potent, even. But the thing is, it's right there, just opposite the church. At night, it's where the drunkards down their bottles and the homeless beg for money and the litter of highs is left behind the morning after, when the children tease each other as they run towards the holy place and the parents call out to them to *Be respectful, come on now!* and the elderly sit beside one another nodding or feeding the pigeons or in absolute silence. And then there's us, climbing this tree in the churchyard where things are holy and sacred and only said in whispers so when we sing quietly we can't hold a tone and it just sounds like we're talking. At least this is what I imagine, when it rains, and all the colors are what others might call dull but are definitely, finally, complete.

*How much Spirit can we hold between us?*
Love is seeking the Spirit of things
together.




Love is
to want for another what is wanted
for oneself.




*I meet myself at my depth*
*so you and I can swim.*



My relationship with Source is the longest,
most intimate and most important I'll ever have.

I am always accompanied, never alone.

*Loved is a sad word for its tense.*
*I believe I will still love bravely.*

— Lotus, my Chinese penpal.

How do I, then, love?

Know that you are worthy of it. So that you are not looking up at your mirror. Stand on the same ground.

I
only
really
care about the tunnels
you've been through,
and
how
you
carry
your
cross.

The priest says to the couple *Did you come here on your own accord? Do you know to your depths what this means, marriage, to love not only when you want to, not only when you feel like it?* I hear him ask and it's like he is asking me, like he is asking me *Do you love when it's uncomfortable to?* Marriage isn't some show. It isn't for the pictures. It is an inner standing. They read their vows from a book and I think of all the lips that have uttered those words from reading those pages over the years, and of all the love left in the ink from those lovers' hearts and of how we are hearing it now. We are hearing the lacing of fingers and the kissing away of years of blame and the dying breaths of pride. From where I'm sitting I only see him. The groom. He's beaming. I know she's smiling already. And when they're told they can kiss he does it five times. *I. loved. you. long. before.*

*Press the middle button until you get a complete sentence:*

And I will hear you at the last hour

and I can tell you that and

I love you a lot.

*I don't do lukewarm love or half spent energy.*
*I am as full as the sun and I'll burn as bright.*

If you think I came all the way here
to experience anything less than open hearted bliss,
you're dead wrong.

*If it is not wholehearted, I do not want it.*

I want to be met by your sincerity
saying I'm softening your soul
and strengthening your heart.
When your favorite part of the day
is the morning, I want you
splayed open and tender. I want you
asking, *How do I surrender in you?*
And until the sun rises once more,
I want to reply.

Love asks what's wrong. Love passes me the water though it's on my side of the bed. He says, *Show me the worst version of you* and dares me to be more enraged, more frightened, more menacing. Love taunts out my fierceness, begs for me to give him my disaster. Love listens to my repentance, to my confession. Love asks for my halves, my pieces; holds my flaws as if they are freckles; and until shame no longer is, love kisses my sin on the lips.

When you truly love someone, you do not project onto them. That would mean that you give them a job: to fulfill your expectation of their behavior. Do they have to act a certain way for you to love them? No. They owe you nothing and are free to do as they please.

When is anything expansive ever expected? Where is the spirit of things born? In the unknown!

So how will you allow the unexpected if you're controlling an outcome? You are avoiding the task that God has given you which is to *serve other people.*

When you project onto someone, you set yourself up for disappointment and leave them open to be hurt by you.

If you truly love someone, you see them for who they are.

It is not you that I am in love with.
It is the way you look at the world and exclaim
*Look at all the shapes the light takes!*
*Look at them all!*

Feed me strawberries in the shower. Draw circles with your fingers on my back to draw out the time. Teach me, with all the feeling from the soles of my feet, to sing. Change my mind about marriage and children. Tell me that for all the dread I hold of the future, the joy they bring isn't worth missing. Tell me you love me. Listen to everything I have to say, even when I forget what that is. Tell me our bedtime story. When we lie together and our breathing becomes the breaking of waves, promise me steady ground. Take your turn to apologize first, and to accept my apology. Promise me a hand to nudge me past myself and eyes that will bring me back. When I get to where I want to be, celebrate with me. Ask me what I mean by looking at you like that. Kiss me when I say I want to marry you and kiss me when I say I want to have your children. Tell me you love me again. Wake me with a hug and touch my hair and whisper *Morning* with your eyes on mine, widening like the sky.

*Open dialogue is where love lives.*

His Spirit sounds different.
His hands are over my eyes
and he has me seeing God.


*You bring out the light in people.*
*Their truth, my truth.*

*I don't know how you do it, but you do.*


It was not the kisses
for me. It was you
perching over the open window
watching the birds welcome the sun,
speaking of the trees.

And as you stood there,
the soft light on your body,
it was the back of your neck
your earlobe, your lashes and a hum
as I joined you in the skylight.

*things are not the same twice*

if you asked me what makes love worth it
i would show you the second before you have to do
something scary and the second
you lock eyes with me

if you asked me what i was thinking
i would place my heart in my mouth and open

if you asked me what my bones feel like
i would wrap your arms around my body and
tell you to squeeze

if you asked me why i want to see you
i would say i haven't been able to yet, and i still do

Tell me I lighten you – empty,
until you're holding onto nothing
that can darken your lens.

Each day from now on is all there is
with your wings around my sternum, and
open arms in reverence.

Show me your Truth without asking.
You said, *I don't know how you do it.*
*Your presence begs I brighten.*




                    Love widens, heightens, reaches.

                    Love sounds like laughter.

                    Love is homeostasis to your nervous system.

                    Love is safety.

When I was fourteen, my History of Art professor left his position at my junior high. My friends and I weren't expecting the lesson on love when he sat down with us to say goodbye.

*Each of you is special,* he said, *and each of you will find the man who will stay by your side. God gave women time. You set the pace. Because when the doors to a woman's heart open, when they bring themselves to a man, they don't close easily. We come for what we want, and we leave. You are here to mold us. You must be like the princess, and he the knight who slays the dragon for you. Have him bring you the head.*

*Now you may be wondering, 'How do you know this teacher?' You don't want to know. You do not want to know.*

I know that my professor, like the legend of the Dragon Slayer, meant for the head of the dragon to be a metaphor for evil being cast out, for the knight to feel he has battled to win the maiden, for him to know he has earned her when she says yes. But I have since learned of a better metaphor still.

To *ride*:

1. sit on and control the movement of (an animal)
2. be carried or supported by (something with a great deal of momentum).

I know ardently that I do not want any murders or graveyards on my land. Not if they can be prevented. Dragons do not intend to harm. They are marvelous creatures, filled with the steam and heat and fire that fills our own hearts. They are protectors. They are guardians. They are symbols of the freedom our fears rabidly tell us are nonexistent, when the existence of freedom itself bears a foundation to the fear. Dragons, like the emotions that live in us, are not to be slain. They are to be invited, welcomed, ridden.

I decide to ask my knight to mount the dragon with me, and steer.

*Accompany another who seeks the same kingdom.*

# **PRAYER**

Please, do not ask me what prayer is. I cannot tell you, for I cannot fit the feeling into words. I am still living the question. At least know, when you hear my broken answer, that it may not mean the same for you.

My grandmother passed in the snow of 2017, and I find myself talking to her on the wind often. *Oma*, we called her. I hear her voice in the song of the seagulls. Some time before, looking out to the boats in the harbor, she had asked me to pray for her in purgatory, and said she'd be praying for me.

I did not know then what prayer was.

The word 'oro' is
Spanish for *gold*
and *I pray*.


*OUR MOUTHS WERE MADE TO SAY PRAYERS.*


When we are aligned,
everything we do is a prayer.

*12 Church Street.* To know the name of something means to have power over it, and I needed a place to call my own. It was here that I learned to listen. I slept on the floor and then on a bed and then on a bed with a frame. We put a great mirror against the wall and called it a living room. I crushed peanut shells between my fingers and tossed them out for the squirrels, only for the birds to eat them. I peered out of my attic bedroom at dawn to see pigeons on the red stone chimneys and heard church bells and thought *how is this not holy?* I stopped hurting for the Earth then. When I realized she didn't need saving. I loved her instead. I sang her the songs I used to sing to my lover. I lit her fires and watered her plants and basked in her sun. I went skinny dipping in her seas and ran barefoot in her forests until nightfall. The barks of her trees bore marks like protective eyes. As if apologizing for an earnest mistake, breath was given each time I took it, and each time I took it, she had more to give.

i pray that my heart may stay where my mouth is

that home remain a safe place never far from reach

that in closing my eyes I'll know where I'm from and it'll be with me

that journeys of a thousand steps may be traveled in tongues

that the word may carry more than a single image

and a memory more feeling than a thought.

Here's to having nothing that can't be said,

to the taboo being lost in the landscape of the heavens.

Prayer is a whisper between lovers. The touch of a feather against the crook of your neck. It is a lifting of the spirit into a darkness where there is nothing left to hold. It is being tickled into screams, a stifling of joy. It is reaching out in disbelief to touch your beard your cheeks your eyes and it is ecstatic laughter. Prayer is forgiveness. It is the dropping of the liquor and of the sword. It is taking a step back so you can take two steps forward. It is a welcoming, a meeting of souls, a surrender. Prayer is closing our eyes to see. It is leaving the mirror face-up for you to hold.

*Tell me where to fall.*

Everything I've whispered to God is a eulogy to a love.

*Let nothing*

*that is not of You*

*be part of me.*

I keep asking God
if you were to leave,
would our love go with you?
Or would I stick my hands through my sleeves
in an attempt to hold its scattering?
Would it belong to me?

But I am one and you another,
our love another still.

This morning,
as the gulls rise on the sea breeze,
my hands fill with shells and
saltwater and words strung into prayer.


I keep asking God
if you were to leave
for my love to go with you.

Be my middle ground, in between
the one who became a woman and the one
who did not know how to be a man.

Be the ground I return to
when my knees buckle
to pray.




I want to open. I want to be full. Love my self to death.
I want to widen, be expanded – in the ways it might at
first hurt. I want to hear my voice. Bold, emboldened
by circumstance and opportunity.




*I am bone-sure that I am being heard,
that I am in constant conversation.*

When I was a child
I wanted someone to be listening
and I know now He always was.

I've counted my losses, then spent them — thrown them over my shoulder. I've piled six months of emotions into an evening, found faith in the ashes of walls faster than I have on an altar, and I've prayed. I've prayed to see what is in front of me, and to not wish things away.

There's a sign at camp
to a *Prayer Facility*
as if sacred words
should be uttered only
in confinement.

But then, they mostly are.

*Prayer is saying what I need to hear be said to me.*

I wish for the mind to quiet and the body to speak.

I choose goodness and healing, even if it's the harder thing to do.

I attract people who see me, truly, and wish for intimacy to be felt, fully, in every relationship in my life.

I wish for light and divinity and faith.

I wish for laughter.

## *WIDE OPEN, WILD & WILLING*

I keep thinking about how much I've changed. My past looked like a series of shackles I kept taking a hammer to until I looked up. There are kids from my school getting married and I wonder how they keep up with each other, I can barely keep up with myself. I hold no secondhand thoughts. I'm growing out of my own height, so devoted to expansion my crown chakra is genuinely gold. I wonder if kings and queens were ever bestowed riches without intact integrity. Surely you're only given such honorary things once your wings are on your body.

*What does being wide open mean to me?*
*What does being wild mean to me?*
*What does being willing mean to me?*

The story goes that

we came from the skies and

planted worlds

                   here

                          and here        and


                                            here.

We are our own ancestors.




What is feral and free

is not a shape.

*I LEARNED THAT I CANNOT CONTROL ANYONE BEYOND MYSELF, AND THAT GOD LIVES IN ME TOO. I LEARNED THAT ACTING IS THE ONLY WAY ANYTHING WILL COME TO ME – I MUST PUT THE WHEEL IN MOTION FIRST. I LEARNED THAT HOW SOMEONE CHOOSES TO FEEL IS NOT SOMETHING I CAN CHANGE. I CAN ONLY CHANGE HOW I CHOOSE TO FEEL. I LEARNED THAT IF I DON'T DRAW THE LINE WHERE I END AND HE BEGINS, AND DEMAND IT REMAIN THERE, THAT HE CAN ATTEMPT TO CROSS IT. I LEARNED THAT ANYONE WHO ATTEMPTS TO CROSS MY LINES DOESN'T BELIEVE IN MY DIVINITY AS I BELIEVE IN THEIRS. I LEARNED THAT EVERYTHING IS MEDICINE WHETHER I CHOOSE TO LET IT HEAL ME OR NOT. I LEARNED THAT WHAT I REPEAT TO MYSELF IS THE FREQUENCY I BECOME AND WHEN IT IS NOT LOVE IT WILL BE ANYTHING ELSE AND WE DO NOT LIVE FOR ANYTHING OTHER THAN LOVE. I LEARNED THAT MY WORTHINESS IS INHERENT IN MY BEING ALIVE. I LEARNED THAT WHO I AM IS MORE SUNSHINE THAN THE SUN ITSELF SOMETIMES BECAUSE I SHARE THROUGH ALL OF MY SENSES AND THAT IS A GOD-GIVEN GIFT.*

There are two types of happiness:

a blissful, ignorant joy, and

an inherent knowledge

that everything will be okay.

Both are equally meaningful.

Tonight, we sit as a family around the fire and my uncle and I are the only ones to see the brightest and longest shooting star and I'll tell you what I wish for because it already came true and it will continue to. I wish for more love.

*i wish for nothing to stop you from fully loving.*

i'm done with counting
the lovers
the mistakes
the kisses with who and when

and i'm back to caring
about every single one
i'm back to rose tinted glasses,
to it all feeling like a lot

i'm back to pointing out the golden sun on the wall
to dancing with the falling leaves
to knowing *this is it*

*We'll reach for heaven
and hold masts to spear the stars.*

Life is a game. It's your move.

# *REMINDERS*

The following pages are notes from the book for you to tear out and stick where you want the reminder, to share with friends, to leave on buses, to use as bookmarks...

*You will become the questions you consider.*

Am I who I need to be for the life I say I want?

*Streamlining.*

Thoughts (Intention)+

Feelings (Intuition) +

Actions & Words (Integrity) +

Results (Presence) =

all Align (Essence).

*The universe matches my momentum.*

You only *must* do what will expand you in *virtue*.

We are to do all things in joy, or not at all.

*Reciprocity* is the natural state of things.

GOD TAKES THE SHAPE OF YOUR EXPECTATIONS.

*How does this*

*o p e n*

*me?*

*People make you feel the way they feel.*

I desire to bring *light* into this world.

WHATEVER YOU DO IS IN SERVICE TO SOMEONE.
*WHO AM I DOING THIS FOR?*

*Am I attached to who I think I am?*

*How has my capacity to*
# *surrender*
*increased?*

I am centered in the sensory feelings of the present moment.

Any form of *self-compassion* can only arise in an environment of *self-responsibility.*

Make your hopes more painful to lose than your fears are pleasant to keep.

YOU
DO
NOT
HAVE
TO
EARN
THE
PLACE
YOU
HAVE
BEEN
GIVEN.

God saw
the outcome
before it began.

# OUR MOUTHS WERE MADE TO SAY PRAYERS.

MY
WORTHINESS
IS INHERENT
IN MY BEING
ALIVE.

Printed in Great Britain
by Amazon